Get a Grip

A Coupon Gift to Put You Back in Charge

SOURCEBOOKS, INC.®
NAPERVILLE, ILLINOIS

Published by Sourcebooks, Inc.
P.O. Box 4410, Naperville, Illinois 60567-4410
(630) 961-3900
FAX: (630) 961-2168
www.sourcebooks.com

ISBN 1-4022-0076-5
Printed and bound in the United States of America
DR 10 9 8 7 6 5 4 3 2 1

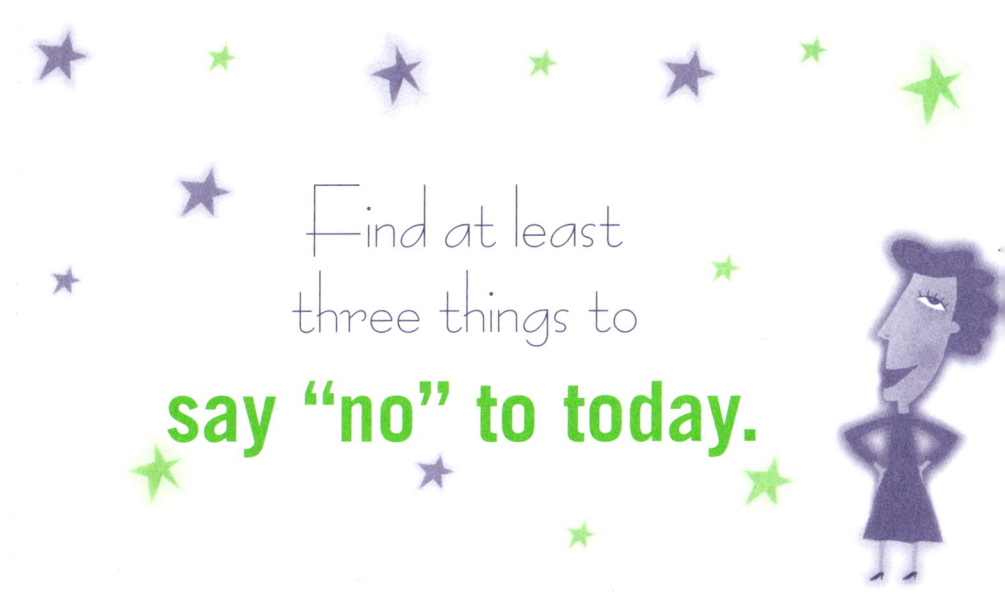

Find at least three things to **say "no" to today.**

This coupon entitles you

to do one thing that you've never done before every day this week. Think "adventure!"

the**Coupon**Collection™

SOURCEBOOKS, INC.
NAPERVILLE, ILLINOIS

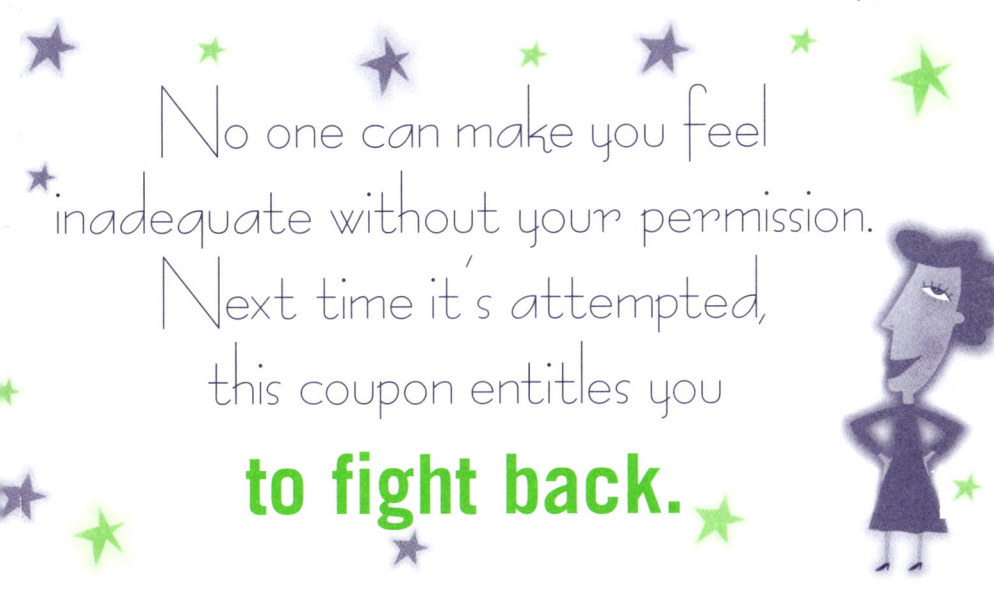

Feeling Overwhelmed?

Take ten minutes to lie flat on your back and breathe from the belly. Set a timer. Think about chocolate.

the**Coupon**Collection™

SOURCEBOOKS, INC.®
NAPERVILLE, ILLINOIS

To Do's

✓ Breathe
✓ Plant flowers
✓ laundry
✓ Post Office
✓ Oil Change
✓ Groceries
✓ redecorate
✓ Exercise
✓ walk the dog
✓ clean the gara
✓ paint house
✓ lawn

Stand before a large mirror and find three things about yourself you adore. Describe them to yourself in glowing detail.

Go through your underwear drawer and throw out anything ratty, ripped, or in any way unworthy of your fabulous self.

the**Coupon**Collection™

SOURCEBOOKS, INC.®
NAPERVILLE, ILLINOIS

To Do's
- ✓ Breathe
- ✓ Plant flowers
- ✓ Laundry
- ✓ Post Office
- ✓ Oil Change
- ✓ Groceries
- ✓ incorporate
- ✓ Exercise
- ✓ Walk the dog
- ✓ Count pr
- ✓ Paint house
- ✓ lawn

Look around your room/house/apartment. Bring in three things that will make you ecstatic.

the**Coupon**Collection™

SOURCEBOOKS, INC.®
NAPERVILLE, ILLINOIS

To Do's

✓ Breathe
✓ Plant flowers
✓ laundry
✓ Post Office
✓ Oil Change
✓ Groceries
✓ redecorate
✓ Exercise
✓ Walk the dog

Somebody upsetting you?

Draw them as a caricature or stick figure, then rip the paper into tiny pieces and toss in the wastebasket. Repeat as necessary.

This coupon will magically make everyone afraid of you.

Treat them gently.

theCouponCollection™

SOURCEBOOKS, INC.®
NAPERVILLE, ILLINOIS

This coupon gives you

permission to burn one piece of paper that upsets you (letter, photo, test, journal entry). If you can't find anything else, burn this coupon.

This coupon gives you

permission to sing for your own pleasure, whether it's in the shower, the car, or in front of an audience.

the**Coupon**Collection™

SOURCEBOOKS, INC.
NAPERVILLE, ILLINOIS

To Do's

✓ Breathe
✓ Plant Flowers
✓ Laundry
✓ Post Office
✓ Oil Change
✓ Groceries
✓ redecorate
✓ Exercise
✓ Walk the dog
✓ Charity pro
✓ clean house
✓ lawn

Commit to something today:
then spend money on it to
seal the deal with yourself.

Present this coupon

to a friend to request one unabashed acknowledgement of your many wonderful qualities.

Need centering?

Visualize yourself as the heart
of a tall, strong tree.
Advice: be an oak or a banyan,
not a palm or a Japanese maple.

Get a grip—

just say no to uncomfortable shoes.

Use this coupon to help you slow down for a moment. Fold it into a paper airplane and find a high place from which to sail it.

This coupon entitles you

to hang up on a tele-marketer without waiting for them to finish. Say, "No thank you" and go back to what you were doing.

This coupon entitles you

to turn down the solicitation
of your choice, guilt-free.

This coupon entitles you

to feel sorry for that snobby salesgirl who forgets that the customer is always right.

theCouponCollection™

SOURCEBOOKS, INC.®
NAPERVILLE, ILLINOIS

To Do's
√ Breathe
√ Plant flowers
√ Laundry
√ Post Office
√ Oil Change
√ Groceries
√ redecorate
√ Exercise
√ Walk the dog
√ Charity
lawn

This coupon entitles you to call a friend and say absolutely everything you have to say on any subject until you're done.

With this coupon,

you will be free from the need to second guess yourself. Say it once.

theCouponCollection™

SOURCEBOOKS, INC.®
NAPERVILLE, ILLINOIS

To Do's
✓ Breathe
✓ Plant flowers
✓ Laundry
✓ Post Office
✓ Oil Change
✓ Groceries
✓ Dry cleaners
✓ Exercise
✓ Walk the dog
✓ Charity
✓ Paint house
✓ Mow lawn

With this coupon, you are entitled to sign up for an auto mechanics course and learn to work on your own car.

With this coupon,

you have permission to do something
entirely out of the ordinary.

the**Coupon**Collection™

SOURCEBOOKS, INC.
NAPERVILLE, ILLINOIS

To Do's

✓ Breathe

✓ Plant flowers

✓ Laundry

✓ Post Office

✓ Oil Change

✓ Groceries

✓ redecorate

✓ Exercise

✓ Walk the dog

✓ Charity

✓ house

✓ lawn

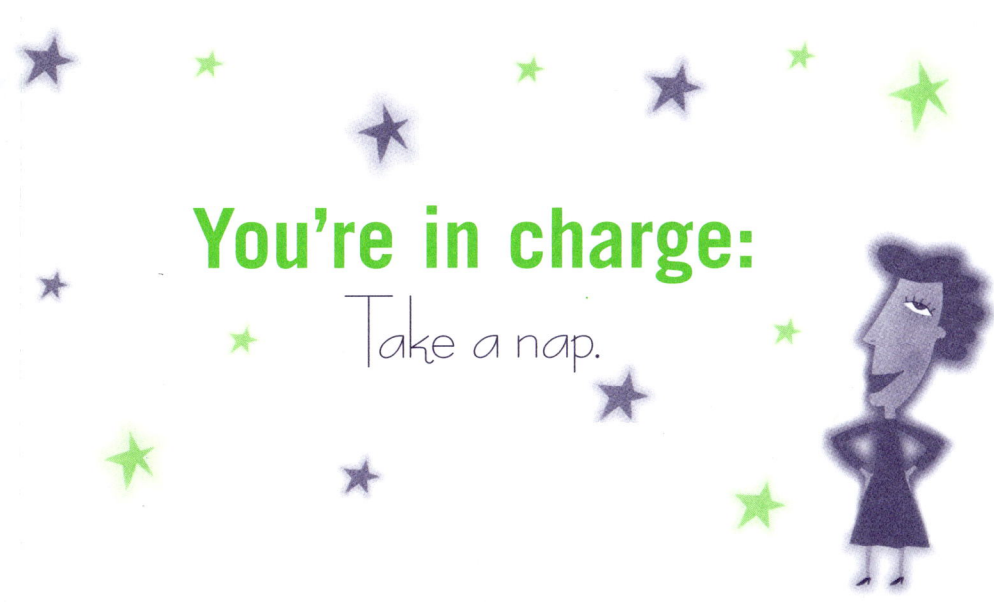

You're in charge:
Take a nap.

This coupon entitles you

to explore a neighborhood, city, or wild place where you've never been. Bring a journal or sketchpad and look for adventures great and small.

theCouponCollection™

SOURCEBOOKS, INC.®
NAPERVILLE, ILLINOIS

To Do's
- ✓ Breathe
- ✓ Plant flowers
- ✓ laundry
- ✓ Post Office
- ✓ Oil Change
- ✓ Groceries
- ✓ pedicure
- ✓ Exercise
- ✓ Walk the dog
- Charity
- paint house
- lawn

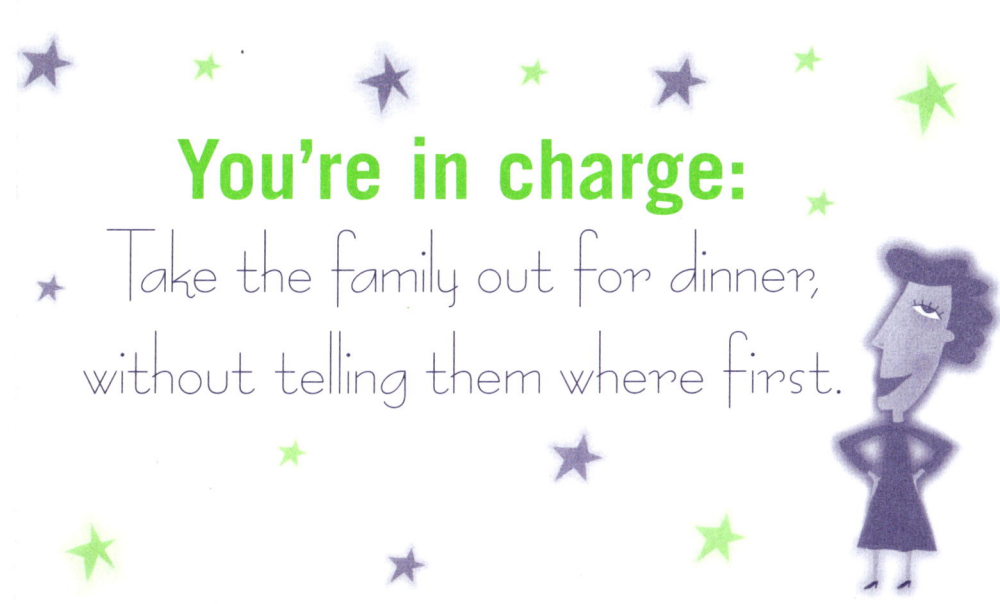

You're in charge:

Take the family out for dinner, without telling them where first.

Present this coupon

to request a completely
straightforward conversation.
No hiding.
Celebrate honesty.

This coupon entitles you

to forget about making
that phone call that you've
been vacillating over.

Use this coupon

when you're suffocating in niceness—
grab a huge pad of paper, or
paint and canvas, and release
some bitchiness and angst.

Celebrate your own competency—spend the evening doing what you do best.

Appreciate yourself fully.

Get a grip—
if you hate your job, leave it or, better yet, transform it.

theCouponCollection™

SOURCEBOOKS, INC.®
NAPERVILLE, ILLINOIS

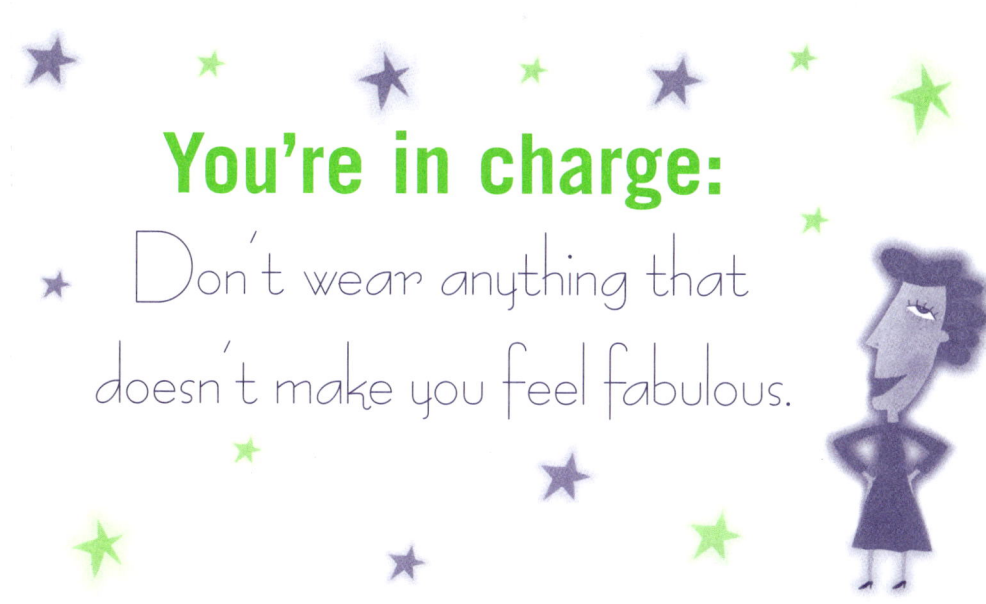

You're in charge:
Don't wear anything that doesn't make you feel fabulous.

Get a grip—

you have the courage to end a

relationship that brings you no joy.

This coupon entitles you

to use the library, Internet, or local college to find out something you always wanted to know.

Get a grip—
hire a cleaning service
once a month.

theCouponCollection™

SOURCEBOOKS, INC.®
NAPERVILLE, ILLINOIS

To Do's

- ✓ Breathe
- ✓ Plant flowers
- ✓ laundry
- ✓ Post Office
- ✓ Oil Change
- ✓ Groceries
- ✓ redecorate
- ✓ Exercise
- ✓ Walk the dog
- ✓ Charity
- house
- lawn

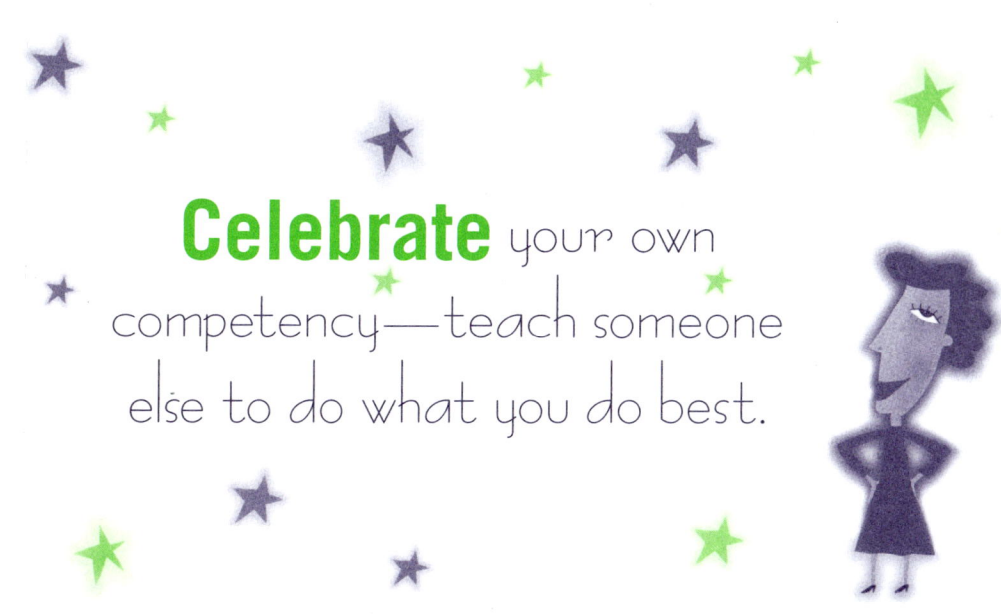

Celebrate your own competency—teach someone else to do what you do best.

Knowledge is power.

Sign up for a course or seminar that will enhance your skill and worth on the job.

theCouponCollection™

SOURCEBOOKS, INC.®
NAPERVILLE, ILLINOIS

To Do's

✓ Breathe
✓ Plant flowers
✓ laundry
✓ Post Office
✓ Oil Change
✓ Groceries
✓ redecorate
✓ Exercise
✓ Walk the dog
✓ charity
✓ clean house
✓ lawn

This coupon entitles you

to be wrong and say so.
If you're too afraid of being
wrong, your life will be very small.

Get a grip—
practice prayer or meditation.

the**Coupon**Collection™

SOURCEBOOKS, INC.®
NAPERVILLE, ILLINOIS

To Do's

✓ Breathe

✓ Plant Flowers

✓ Laundry

✓ Post Office

✓ Oil Change

✓ Groceries

✓ redecorate

✓ Exercise

✓ Walk the dog

✓ Clean ...

Find inspiration in history—
read about the lives of
other fabulous women.

Get a grip—
get yourself the best
haircut you can afford.

theCouponCollection™

SOURCEBOOKS, INC.®
NAPERVILLE, ILLINOIS

To Do's

✓ Breathe

✓ Plant flowers

✓ laundry

✓ Post Office

✓ Oil Change

✓ Groceries

✓ redecorate

✓ Exercise

✓ Walk the dog

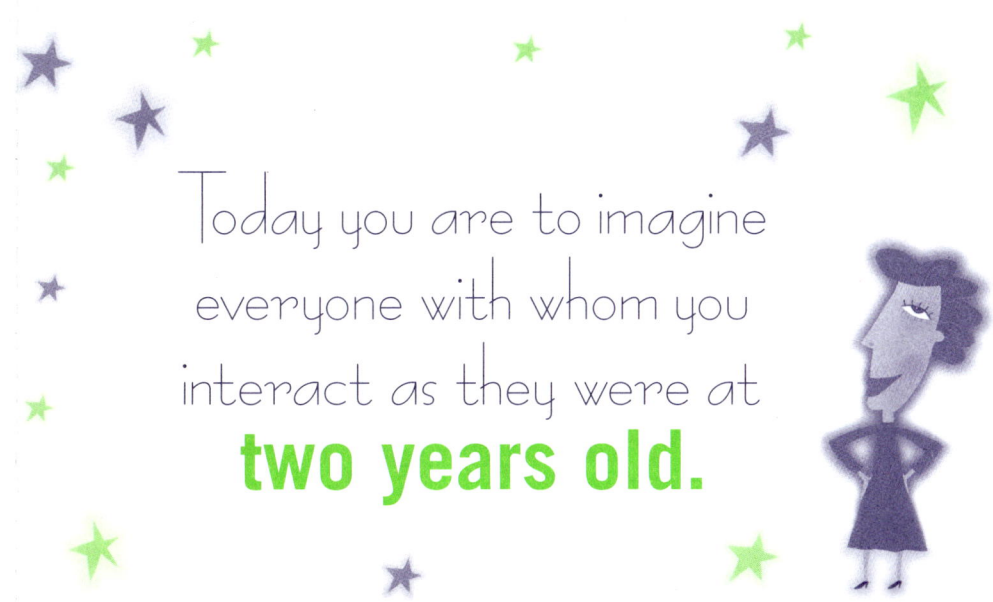

Today you are to imagine everyone with whom you interact as they were at **two years old.**

Be a hearty and
resourceful traveler.
Envision the perfect adventure,
research it, plan it to the last
detail; then take a deep
breath and embark.

theCouponCollection™

SOURCEBOOKS, INC.®
NAPERVILLE, ILLINOIS

∞ a breath of fresh air ∞

Get a Grip: A Coupon Gift to Put You Back in Charge

The Wild Side of Womanhood: A Coupon Gift to Unleash Your Audacious Power

The Goddess Within: A Coupon Gift that Celebrates You

Going Over the Hill Slowly: A Coupon Gift That Keeps You Young

Available at your local gift store or bookstore or by calling (800) 727-8866.

Collect them all!

✑ from me to you ✑

I Love You Dad: A Coupon Gift of Love and Thanks
I Love You Mom: A Coupon Gift of Love and Thanks
Dear Grad: A Coupon Gift of Congratulations
Best of Friends: A Coupon Gift of Love and Thanks

✑ the country life ✑

I Love You Grandma: A Unique Tear-Out Coupon Gift of Love and Thanks
Dear Mom: A Unique Tear-Out Coupon Gift Just for You
Country Cat: A Unique Tear-Out Coupon Gift for the Feline Lover
A Country Life Wherever You Are: A Unique Tear-Out Coupon Gift for a Simpler Life

Available at your local gift store or bookstore or by calling (800) 727-8866.

Collect them all!

∞ a gift for the spirit ∞

Simple Serenity: A Coupon Gift to Help and Support You
A Little Bit of Feng Shui: A Coupon Gift to Gently Shift Your Energies
A Little Bit of Yoga: A Coupon Gift to Energize and Relax You
Living in Abundance: A Coupon Gift to Enhance and Enrich You

∞ a drop of sunshine ∞

Slow Down: A Book of Peaceful Coupons
Faith, Hope and Love: A Coupon Gift to Restore Your Spirit
Angels: A Coupon Gift of Miracles
The Artist in You: A Coupon Gift to Spark Your Creativity

Available at your local gift store or bookstore or by calling (800) 727-8866.

Collect them all!